In *Praying Our Way Toward W*[barcode] out to establish that "Life is the greatest grace. He explains easy-to-understand language how a real life of prayer comes about—through faithfulness to daily personal prayer, no matter what the odds, and surrendering to God's action of purification and transformation of the human person.

SISTER MARY MARTIN, O CARM, RETIRED DIRECTOR OF
LAY CARMELITES, PROVINCE OF THE PURE HEART OF MAY

✳ ✳ ✳

Praying Our Way Toward Wholeness is the fruit of years of contemplative wisdom, much theological reflection and prayer, and fifty-five years of priestly ministry, most of which were spent working with those who have slipped through the cracks and in some cases, in the words of Pope Francis, have been "thrown away. This book should be read by all who experience discontent with both life and religion and who are willing to venture a challenging journey to the center.

DONALD BUGGERT, O CARM, PROFESSOR EMERITUS,
WASHINGTON THEOLOGICAL UNION

✳ ✳ ✳

With a keen eye, Father Tracy explores the wisdom about prayer in the Scriptures and the liturgy and in the wisdom he has gained from his long experience serving those whom society has neglected. You will soon find a reason every day to turn to the wisdom of this gifted spiritual guide.

KEITH J. EGAN, T O CARM, UNIVERSITY OF NOTRE DAME
AND SAINT MARY'S COLLEGE

In a world marked by brokenness and the loneliness of individuals by indifference to silence and contemplation, and the search for technological solutions to human problems, the pastoral witness of an authentic consecrated life is of great value to the church and the world. Intimacy is rooted in constant and profound conversation with God. *Praying Our Way Toward Wholeness* is an excellent reminder that the message from our merciful God is always "Love."

BERNADETTE MOORE GIBSON, DIRECTOR OF PASTORAL CARE
AT OLD ST. PATRICK'S CHURCH, CHICAGO

Now more than ever, we need to do all that we can to help youth and young adults enter into a life of prayer and meditation. So many of them feel lost and lonely. They are many times confused and suffer from hopelessness. Father Tracy's *Praying Our Way Toward Wholeness* will be a wonderful practical guide to this deeper encounter with Jesus, who walks with us on the journey.

✝ DAVID O'CONNELL, AUXILIARY BISHOP OF LOS ANGELES,
SAN GABRIEL REGION

PRAYING OUR WAY TOWARD WHOLENESS

TRACY O'SULLIVAN, O.CARM.

PRAYING OUR WAY TOWARD WHOLENESS

A STEP-BY-STEP GUIDE TO
daily prayer

TWENTY-THIRD PUBLICATIONS
twentythirdpublications.com

Author Tracy O'Sullivan hosts a weekly blog
(available in both English and Spanish)
dedicated to supporting you on your spiritual journey.

Visit **www.prayingalonetogether.blogspot.com**
as well as his pages on Facebook:
www.facebook.com/Tracy.OsullivanO.Carm
and **www.facebook.com/tracyocarm**

Twenty-Third Publications
One Montauk Avenue, Suite 200
New London, CT 06320
(860) 437-3012 or (800) 321-0411
www.twentythirdpublications.com

Copyright © 2019 Tracy O'Sullivan, O. Carm. All rights reserved.
No part of this publication may be reproduced in any manner without prior
written permission of the publisher. Write to the Permissions Editor.

Cover photo: iStock.com/DJClaassen

ISBN: 978-1-62785-446-7
Library of Congress Control Number: 2018962497
Printed in the U.S.A.

 A division of Bayard, Inc.

CONTENTS

SECTION TWO: CONTEMPLATION

INTRODUCTION

EVERYONE WANTS TO BE HAPPY. God made the heart with that most fundamental hunger. Our problem is finding what makes us happy for the long run. Our faith tells us that the simple answer is walking with Jesus. The difficulty is that life has so many deceptions and illusions that it is hard to find the true Jesus.

Jesus is the Word of God. All we want to know about God will be found in Jesus. All that God has done and is doing for the world is revealed in Jesus. The Scriptures tell us God's message and God's intentions for us. At both the deepest level and at the simplest level, they are an expression of love. Jesus pulls all the various themes and stories of the Bible together in his life, death, and resurrection. In that love story in Jesus, we are invited to find the purpose of our life. If we do find it and embrace it, we will possess the happiness that does not slip away.

One of the best ways to encounter Jesus is unswerving commitment to deep personal prayer. In this prayer, the emphasis is to change our lives—not to change God to meet our desires. I will explain this type of prayer in the context of Carmelite spirituality. The Carmelite tradition teaches us that God loves us first and loves us as we are in all our brokenness. This is the beginning point for all prayer.

Our growth in prayer begins with the effort of our mind and imagination. They help us get in touch with God. As the growth progresses, there is a process of purification and transformation beyond our effort, leading to union with God. This special intervention by God is called contemplation.

In the experience of contemplation there is a switch of focus to God's part in prayer. The mind, the heart, and the entire being need to be prepared for this new reality. Our perception and, even more, our experience of God, as well as our understanding of self, must undergo a radical makeover. This produces a feeling of turmoil. Our sense of clarity and security in things spiritual crumbles. This is good. Surrender and acceptance are the way forward.

St. John of the Cross says, "Contemplation is none other than a secret, peaceful and loving infusion of God, which, if the soul allows it to happen, infuses a spirit of love" (*Dark Night*, I.10.6).

This book is an effort to make deep personal prayer understandable and attractive. It is a call to pray regularly. This will only happen with a personal discipline. In Section One I describe what this prayer is. I also present two practical methods of prayer. The following chapters delve into the foundations, benefits, obstacles, and difficulties in prayer.

In Section Two I talk about the call to contemplation, which is a gift from God usually related to our progress in prayer. I present Teresa of Ávila's teachings on seeking contemplation from her classic, *The Interior Castle.*

Prayer is a journey. Each of us has our own place on the journey. This book will help you identify where you are and encourage you to move on. It is helpful to all of us if we understand that we all share the need for a good GPS when it comes to prayer. None of us are totally secure in our directions. The Carmelite tradition is a special roadmap created by some of the great saints and doctors of the church. It is a call for beginners, a lift for those on the way, and an awesome guide for those approaching home. One thing we all share is that we need to take the next step. Hopefully, this text will help you discover what is next for you in walking with Jesus in prayer.

SECTION ONE

Prayer

One

REFLECTIONS
ON PRAYER

WHEN TALKING ABOUT DEEP PERSONAL PRAYER I AM USING THOMAS MERTON'S DEFINITION and the added insights of Teresa of Ávila. Merton says:

> Prayer then means yearning for the simple presence
> of God, for a personal understanding of God's word,
> for knowledge of God's will, and for the capacity to
> hear and obey God.

Teresa says prayer "is nothing else than an intimate sharing between friends; it means taking time frequently to be alone with Him who we know loves us." All prayer must raise our awareness of God's loving presence. Humility is the foundation of prayer. It moves us to realize our total dependence on God.

We need to engage God's word. The most privileged way of this encounter is in the Bible but also in the experiences of our life. This interaction of life and prayer will be a theme throughout this text. The encounter with God's word leads us to what God wants, a call out of our selfishness to generosity toward God and others. In this prayer, listening is the key. New insights into the reality of how God guides our way of living open new horizons for humility, service, and love. This dialogue is rooted in God's love for us.

Committed personal prayer comes in many different forms: vocal, mental, meditation, *lectio divina*, and contemplative prayer. This dedication to prayer requires a discipline to pray on a regular basis. Committed personal prayer is an effort to bring prayer into life habitually, no matter how we feel. It might start out as only several minutes a day, but with faithfulness, discipline, and generosity it will grow. It will gradually transform our lives. It leads us in a journey to be totally in love with God.

FIVE POINTS OF PRAYER

There are five important points in Merton's definition of prayer:

- The first is that we focus on the presence of God. This demands a conscious effort to direct our attention to an experience of the sacred.

- Second, we bring God's word into our mind, seeking understanding.

- Third, this reflection should lead us to a sense of what God wants of us.

- Fourth, we bring this insight to our life so the word speaks to us and leads us forward.

- In the fifth step, we live in obedience to God's call. Prayer is all about life and the way we live.

Later, I will explain two prominent forms of prayer: *lectio divina* and Christian Meditation. Here, I will briefly use *lectio divina* to further explain prayer in a more general way. *Lectio divina* is a prayerful reading of the Bible or, at times, reflection on a profound personal experience.

As we begin committed personal prayer, the first item is to gather ourselves so that we can pay attention to the fact that we are in the loving presence of God.

The heart is the deepest truth about us. The Bible speaks of the heart almost a thousand times. It is the heart that is the source of prayer. The heart is where we encounter our most real self.

The four steps of *lectio divina* are reading, reflecting, responding, and resting. The first steps, reading and reflection, may take the majority of the time in the first stages of this new personal prayer. However, the job of reading and reflection is to bring us to a deeper sense of God's presence. The last two steps are praying with an open heart and resting in silence in the loving presence of the one we know loves us.

In sum, prayer is gathering all our faculties to pay attention to the intimate presence of God, to seek a loving and life-giving encounter with God. We have a sense of a sacred presence calling us to life in love. This experience of committed personal prayer seeks to clarify the will of God in the concrete reality of our daily experience. True prayer empowers us to bring God's love to our life in service of the kingdom.

> "Listen, I am standing at the door knocking; if you
> hear my voice and open the door, I will come in to
> you and eat with you, and you with me."
>
> ✳ **REVELATION 3:20**

The single greatest obstacle to prayer is to not begin. The second is the relentless attack of distractions. The resolution of distractions is an ongoing problem that needs much attention, but ultimately, it is a return to our focal point.

THE HIDDEN TREASURE

Scripture helps us delve more deeply into the gift of prayer. The parable of the lost treasure (Matthew 13:44–46) is a fruitful example. There are three steps in this parable: finding the treasure, selling all we have, and buying the field.

The "finding" comes from a sense of hunger in the depths of the heart, a feeling of incompleteness. There is a recognition that life holds more than what we have. In the "finding" we often experience God's love for us in our brokenness.

The "selling" involves making a commitment to pray. This costs us our time and comfort. Creating a schedule, building an atmosphere, and discovering and practicing a method of prayer all come at a cost: self-sacrifice. What we are doing is making space for God by letting go on God's terms.

The "buying" brings us to the practice of prayer as a regular and disciplined part of our lifestyle. We address the issues that are hindering our pursuit of God.

The initial atmosphere for prayer is important. We need to minimize distractions by seeking the most silence and solitude that is a practical reality for us. For some, a candle or incense or religious art is helpful. We need to be aware of who it is we are encountering. Second, prayer always has to be rooted in love responding to love. Third, prayer needs to come from a heart yearning for faithfulness to love.

All prayer must begin with a sense of the loving presence of God. The material we read and the thoughts that lead to reflection almost always have a spark of light, sometimes quite intense. This touches our spirit and calls us to change. This is our own metro center that carries us from the mind to the heart and into life.

Prayer is about how we live, not how we feel. Most often, God gives beginners at prayer a sense of peace and progress. Gradually, God weans us from the beautiful feelings to sharpen our focus away from ourselves and toward God.

SELF-KNOWLEDGE

Genuine self-knowledge, which opens us up to our true self, always helps our prayer. It invites us to get real. In turn, when our prayer is authentic, we get to know ourselves more truthfully. A major purpose of prayer is to draw us out of a world of self-deception, illusions, and a sense of self-importance that places us at the center of our world. The slow process of growing in self-knowledge leads to that gradual development of personal transformation called conversion, which is repeated at several levels. The journey to refocus and recognize God at the center is only possible when we acknowledge our sinfulness and selfishness.

With faithfulness to prayer there are changes. We slowly grow in patience. The possibilities of reconciliation come out of nowhere. Situations where it was difficult to see the other side of a story now often open up to four or five different valid points of view. The prejudices of a lifetime get exposed for exactly what they are—a lie. We become more sensitive to the needs of the poor and issues of justice. We see the conflict between our lifestyle and a responsible care for the environment, such as recycling and the appropriate use of water and energy. This is the dynamic beginning of our pilgrimage to God with Jesus leading the way.

Having considered the overall message of prayer, we will now address two practical methods of prayer.

Two

TWO METHODS OF PRAYER

THE PRAYERFUL READING OF THE BIBLE: *LECTIO DIVINA*
VATICAN II BROUGHT THE WORD OF GOD IN THE BIBLE TO THE CENTER OF ALL CHRISTIAN SPIRITUALITY. This revival has led to a growing practice of prayer that has had a long tradition in the church. This is called *lectio divina*. Literally, this means divine reading. A more accurate description would be the prayerful reading of the Bible.

This prayerful reading seeks to listen to what God has to say to us. It will lead us to know and embrace God's will. It is all about the transforming encounter with God's special means of revelation, the Hebrew and Christian Scriptures.

When approaching the Mystery unveiled in the Scriptures, we need the attitude of Samuel: "Speak, Lord, your servant is listening" (1 Samuel 3:10).

There are four steps to this prayerful reading of the Bible:

1. A slow meditative *reading* of a selected text of the Scriptures.

2. A *reflection* on the text that connects it with our life experience.

3. A *response* in prayer to this reflective activity.

4. Finally, a quiet *resting* in the Mystery of this encounter.

THE FOUR STEPS

It is essential to prepare for this serious time of prayer. We need to create an ambiance of silence, with minimal outside distractions. Next, we select the text. We then invoke the Holy Spirit.

1. In the initial step, we have to seek out the meaning: What does the text say? Silence is important for listening and avoiding the trap of making the text say what we want. We need to bring the heart into the process as well as the mind. A particular phrase

or sentence may burst out as a light, sometimes gently, sometimes with great force. Hold on to it.

2. In the second step, we want to ask: What does the text say to us? We enter into a dialogue with the text. Here we want to make the connection to our life. The reflection leads to building a bridge between God's word and our life situation at this moment. In this process, the distractions will never be far away. To cast out these chattering monkeys in the mind, always return to the text. This discipline maintains a recollected and focused approach to the task of reflection in the second step.

3. In the third step, we try to discover what the text leads us to say to God. We are moved to prayer. We speak to God of how we know we want to change, but it is a struggle. We cannot do it by ourselves. Honesty is the true gold of this form of prayer. We seek support in healing a flawed relationship or getting rid of a bad habit. We ask help and guidance. We make resolutions to be more generous in walking with Jesus. Patience is truly important. This is always a slow journey from the head to the heart to life. This is about self-knowledge, a topic considered at length in later chapters.

4. The fourth step, quiet listening and resting in the Lord, generates a contemplative mood. This is the goal of the prayerful reading of the Bible: opening ourselves up to the transforming love of God. Silence is the language of God. We slowly grow in the wonder that God loves us. While we do not always have this deep encounter of loving silence, it remains the goal. It is the gift that transforms us into the image of Christ.

SPIRITUAL TRANSFORMATION

When we approach the prayerful reading of the Bible in *lectio divina*, we should see ourselves as the one to whom the Bible is directed. It was formulated to address us here and now. However, we are always a member of a community.

Our search for the meaning of the Scriptures needs to include the church's guidance in biblical studies. Praying the Scriptures should lead us to seek an understanding of the biblical meaning. Prayer and study need to steer us away from making the Bible fit our demands and desires.

We need to keep the concrete reality of our life, our family, our community, and the larger circumstances of the political, economic, and social reality front and center. The Bible is at all times the book of the community, not a personal prayer book.

The first three steps are an encounter with Christ-for-us. He is our Savior calling us to new life. In the final and most important step we meet Christ-in-us. This presence grows in the gradual transformation of our being when we are faithful and generous to our prayerful reading of the Bible. We are truly walking with Jesus.[1]

CHRISTIAN MEDITATION

Christian Meditation centers on silence. It is a contemplative approach. It hopes to eliminate all thinking and the imagination during the period of prayer. The silence invites God to be active in our prayer. The spirit of poverty is the goal. We simply seek to create an emptiness that is the best invitation to the Spirit, where God prays within us.

The individual is asked simply to silently repeat the holy word *maranatha*, which means "the Lord will come." The choice of the word is arbitrary, and it is important not to think of its meaning. The repetition connects to one's breathing. The slow repetition of the word is the individual's prayer.

The simple and slow repetition of the mantra has a clear goal: the creation of silence. This happens by drawing the focus away from the mind and imagination. These are the source of the distractions. There is a fear on the part of the ego that the silence will mean the loss of the ego's control. Simplicity needs to be the goal. The gentle repetition of the mantra frees us to let go. We want to open space for God.

---

1   This material is deeply dependent on Carlos Mesters, O. Carm., who has spent a lifetime of making biblical scholarship meaningful for the poor of Latin America.

The repeating of the word symbolizes and encourages the faithful surrender to God. The important issue is to grow in purity of heart with openness to God's grace.

The prayer is experiential and practical. People need to start the journey and let the experience be the teacher. Through the simple repetition of the mantra, *maranatha*, we clear the mind, get beyond thinking. We move from the head to the heart. We need to pay attention to how we say the mantra. Our effort should be calm but firm in our prayerful repetition. This clears the mind enough to make space for the Spirit. We must realize the final measure of effective prayer is a life more in tune with the values of the gospel, walking with Jesus.

HOW TO MEDITATE

The most important thing to learn about meditation is to meditate. It is extraordinarily simple. This is the problem. Few believe that something so simple is so effective and transforming.

To meditate, sit still and upright while seeking the awareness of God's presence. As you relax, close your eyes. Slowly begin saying the mantra in four syllables. Do not think or imagine anything. As distractions come, return to the mantra softly but decisively. Even good thoughts are to be excluded. The target is twenty to thirty minutes in the morning and evening.

There are three simple goals to guide the two meditation periods each day:

1. Say the mantra for the complete time of the meditation. This is a skill. It will take time to create a habit.

2. Say the mantra throughout the meditation without interruption. The task here is to continually return as soon as possible from the persistent distractions that are the ego's hunger for control.

3. In saying the mantra, let it draw you into the depths of your being, beyond thought, imagination, and all images. Rest in the presence of God dwelling in the depth of your heart.

MEDITATION TODAY

Different forms of meditation are growing in popularity today. Most of them are rooted in personal well-being. Christian Meditation has a totally different agenda. The gospel is not about self-analysis but self-transcendence. Christian Meditation happens only when we shift attention away from ourselves. The irony of this approach is that it leads to deeper and more authentic self-knowledge.

Christian Meditation enriches but does not replace other prayers, such as *lectio divina*, the liturgy, spiritual reading, or the Rosary and other devotions. Christian Meditation is a foundation for a rich and committed spiritual life. If practiced daily over a period of time, noticeable changes occur.

Faithfulness to Christian Meditation is an anchor for a spiritual life that opens one's heart to surrender to God.

Christian Meditation is not magic. If you are looking for the easy fix, you will not find it. However, faithful practice of this prayer will lead you to purity of heart and surrender to God. Gospel values seep into one's heart and mind. There is a new light and love in all we encounter. Christian Meditation, if practiced dutifully and with generosity, is a sure way to walk in the footsteps of Jesus Christ.[2]

PRACTICAL SUGGESTIONS

When I introduce this spiritual technique, I make the following points:

- It does not matter if you feel at peace, even though this often is the case for beginners. How you feel is not the issue. The real issue is change in your heart that leads to a better life.

- It often seems as if our mind is locked into unyielding distractions. You need to peacefully return to the mantra and continue repeating it

---

2   Ernest Larkin, O. Carm., *Contemplative Prayer for Today: Christian Meditation* (Mediomedia, Singapore, 2007). Larkin's message is that the teachings and practices of Christian Meditation as proposed by Father John Main, OSB, are totally compatible with the long and illustrious Carmelite tradition of prayer and spirituality.

slowly and steadily. Let the monkeys that are the distractions play on.

- It is important to reject all thoughts, including good and inspiring ideas. There is another time for them but not during this sacred time seeking the loving presence of God in silence.

- Always remember that prayer is fundamentally an act of love for God. As Teresa of Ávila said, we need not think much but we need to love much.

- In the end, it comes down to discipline. One has to make time twice a day for twenty to thirty minutes. The practice can easily be put off and eventually will slip away.

I have presented two methods of prayer with the hope you will use them soon and regularly. Prayer is an experience. It grows with practice. It opens new horizons but also new questions and concerns. When we pray, there are several items that can help or hinder our prayer. The following chapters will provide direction to avoid the pitfalls and direct the way forward in peace and light. We begin with reflection on why the Bible works so well in helping our prayer.

Three

THE BIBLE
AND PRAYER
Why the Bible Inspires Us

THE PEOPLE'S EXPERIENCE OF GOD

IN MY CLASS RECENTLY, A HUSBAND ARRIVED LATE AND GAVE A SHORT, AFFECTIONATE KISS TO HIS WIFE as he sat down next to her. That kiss was quite simple yet very complicated. It was not just an expression of affection but the consequence of many decades together for better or worse, in sickness and in health.

The Bible is like that kiss. It is a love story of God and his people. It is both simple and clear but also complicated and wrapped up in a story of human frailty covering centuries.

The story is about the call and promise made to Abraham. It is the story of salvation, the liberation from consequences of sin revealed in the first eleven chapters of Genesis. The story covers almost two thousand years, leading to Jesus.

In its broadest sweep, the story flows from Abraham to Moses to David to the prophets, and then it climaxes in Jesus. It is a continual expression of God's faithfulness and human ambivalence. The story moves from the promise of Abraham becoming the father of a great nation to Moses liberating the people on the way to the Promised Land. The era of David and the kings initiates the idea of hope for God's final intervention in the person of the Messiah. The enlightenment of the prophets' message expands and deepens this hope. It also draws us deeper into the mystery of this ever-active and saving God.

During this entire journey of Abraham's family, the hope of the promise evolves in spite of the consistent and profound infidelity of the people. Likewise, there is a continual growth in understanding of who God is and what God wants. Many centuries after Abraham, the people came to the singular awareness that there is only one God: the God of Abraham, of Isaac, and of Jacob.

The entire thrust of the movement of salvation history leads to Jesus, the Word of God. In Jesus we have the fullness of God's revelation. We have the invitation into the

Mystery of Love. There is a beautiful harmony between the Jewish Scriptures and the great event of Christ crucified and Christ risen.

This story of the Bible, the story of salvation, was put together by the people reflecting, sharing, and praying about their experience of God. Most of the writings in the Bible are the conclusion of the community's deep discernment over a long period of time of their encounter with God in their lives. This was a steady process of maturing where the gentle guidance of the Holy Spirit directed the journey leading to Jesus, the final and complete Word of God in the flesh.

A centerpiece of this journey for God's people was the Exodus: the liberation from slavery, the passage through the desert, and the entry into the Promised Land. The power of this experience guided the people all through an often-torturous history. Again, and again, the children of Abraham reflected on the faithfulness of God setting them free. They found strength and fortitude in encountering the revelation of this God of the Exodus in their present troubled plight.

The same is true of the death and resurrection of Jesus. This ultimate expression of God's saving love has become the gateway to the new day, the New Exodus, in Christian history.

The central point of the story of salvation in the Bible is that the message in all its breadth and depth comes from the people's experience of God active in their lives and their history. The power and significance of the Bible are that the same God of the Chosen People is in our life. The word in the Bible is the light that enables us to encounter, understand, and embrace the reality of God's continuing presence in our life. We are invited to participate in the call and promise, the pilgrimage through history to the kingdom of God. The gift of God's word in the revelation of the Bible is always a call to new life and new horizons.

STUDY AND PRAYER

Our approach to the Bible requires two distinct methods. One is to study the Bible to absorb the story and to grow in familiarity with the word of God. This should be done prayerfully, but basically it is an exercise of study. The second approach is the prayerful reading of the Scriptures. This task goes beyond the mind to the depth of the spirit within us. This is a truly different tactic. This has three points of importance:

1. to be the seed that falls into the ground to die only to sprout to new life and bear the fruit of God's kingdom by our surrender to God's call and listening to what God has to say to us;

2. to learn God's will;

3. to be more committed to walk with Jesus.

This is done in the context of our experience and especially of our problems, both personal and in society. In this prayerful reading of the Bible, we need to encounter the word as if it is addressed to us personally.

We need to always be aware that the text is more than a fact. It is a symbol, a window, that lets us see the past as a mirror of today's experience. This prayerful reading of the word of God needs to lead us into our present historical reality to unveil the mystery of God's saving presence right here and now.

UNION WITH GOD

> The word of God is something alive and active: it cuts like any double-edged sword but more finely; it can slip though the place where the soul is divided from the spirit, or joints from the marrow; it can judge the secret emotions and thoughts. No created thing can hide from him; everything is uncovered and open to the eyes of the one to whom we must give account of ourselves. ＊ HEBREWS 4:12–13

The call is central to the Bible's story of salvation. From Abraham to Jesus, the call is always a principal part of the message. As the clarity of the message evolves, the purpose of the call finally arrives at its conclusion—to be one with God. This union with God is the shared and final destiny of all God's children.

As we steadily become more aware through prayer, especially *lectio divina*, of how God is clearly and convincingly in our lives, there are consequences for us. God always wants more and is working to transform us in the image of his Son. This call to change is never easy. This is at the heart of our work for spiritual maturity.

The word of God is indeed a two-edged sword. It opens a part of our life that we strive hard to keep hidden. We are called by the word expressed in the Bible and in our life experience to be the seed that falls into the ground to die only to sprout to new life and bear the fruit of God's kingdom by our surrender to God's call.

This exposure to God in our life brings us to an awareness of our limits and sinfulness. It opens a journey of self-knowledge that is the absolute foundation to growth in prayer. We will consider this topic of self-knowledge in our next chapter.

four

WHY SELF-KNOWLEDGE IS IMPORTANT IN PRAYER

GOD RESIDES AT THE DEEPEST CENTER OF EVERY HUMAN BEING. Prayer is a journey to that center. The encounter with God's word and will is our ticket to the center. Prayer is an invitation to use God's word and will to refocus our lives. The light of the Scriptures often opens new horizons in our normal awareness. This leads to deeper self-knowledge.

Our normal world is filled with false values, illusions, and a grandiose sense of self-importance. They all join together to blind us to God's presence in the depths of our heart. Clearing this passage is the task of an authentic spiritual life. Self-knowledge is a crucial element on this path.

Giving such importance to self-knowledge may seem strange to you. To make this more understandable I would like to invite you to look at your life today compared to five or ten or fifteen years ago. If you have worked at living your faith minimally, I am sure you can see a lot of changes. Self-knowledge was an important part of that maturing process. More patience, more tolerance, and more reconciliation are all woven into the larger progression of knowing ourselves with growing clarity. This new wisdom leads to an expanding awareness of our dependence on God.

In our time, psychological self-knowledge is a major industry that contributes to our well-being. Likewise, Al-Anon and all other twelve-step programs and their affiliates are rooted in self-knowledge. These major initiatives can be part of our spiritual journey.

Most of the Gospel mandates flow from this practice of refocusing to put God at the center:

> "If anyone wants to be first, he must make himself last of all." ✳ MARK 9:35

> "Whoever finds his life will lose it, and whoever loses his life for my sake will find it." ✳ MATTHEW 10:39

"Whoever wishes to come after me must deny himself, take up his cross and follow me." * MATTHEW 16:24

"Unless a grain of wheat falls to the ground and dies, it remains a grain of wheat; but if it dies, it produces much fruit." * JOHN 12:24

The journey of self-knowledge is often described as moving from the false self to the true self. It is a new way of looking at ourselves, at others, and at the world. It is a transformation of consciousness.

The false self is entrenched in our exaggerated sense of self-importance, our illusions of grandiosity, the blindness of our addictions, and, most of all, the unreality of our idols. Our heart creates many false centers in our attachments, including the distorted use of God's creatures. The heart becomes fragmented and flawed.

We tend to become blinded to our faults and failures. We emphasize the shortcomings of others. Jesus put it ever so clearly when he pointed out our blindness: we stress the splinter in our neighbor's eye rather than the log in our eye (Matthew 7:4–5). Self-righteousness rises to the front and center. As we become aware of the false values flowing from our fragmented heart, we come to a fork in the road.

We have a choice of life or death. We choose death when we double down on the clamoring of the false self. We choose life when we open ourselves to the mercy of God, which leads to the true self. At the heart of this encounter is the perennial challenge of knowing ourselves.

SELF-KNOWLEDGE OPENS TO GOD'S MERCY

Even the simplest things in life are often misled by the false self. Having the right kind of clothes, a nice home, the lifestyle of our proper state, and a good reputation are all potentially innocent choices. The false self has a field day refocusing these items to contribute to a deceitful vision of self-importance. Companies spend billions of dollars on advertising to encourage us to feed the exaggerated demands of the false self. The unending pulls of a consumer society are a singular and horrendous obstacle on the road to the true self. All these deviations work together to weaken, and even hide, the longing of the true self calling us to move on to the center in a more authentic life. This blockage is especially powerful when the distortions flow from an addiction that becomes rooted not only in the psychological system of the person but also in the nervous system of the body. This is the case in the abuse of alcohol, drugs, sex, and gambling, to name the chief culprits.

Here again, self-knowledge, an awareness of what is going on within us, is critical in the necessary conversion that comes when we hear God's word and obey God's will in prayer.

St. Teresa of Ávila received this message from God: "Seek yourself in me." She came to understand that God accepts us as we are. She pointed out the brokenness of

Mary Magdalene, the Canaanite woman, and her favorite, the Samaritan woman at the well. Jesus did not send them off to a thirty-day retreat and wait until they were perfect. No, Jesus encountered them as they were. He called them in the midst of their weakness and faults. He does the same for us.

For Teresa, self-knowledge led to two important facts that became the foundation of all her spirituality. In the first, she saw her distracted heart pulled in many directions leading away from God. In this fragmented heart she identified her sinfulness. Likewise, she slowly accepted her helplessness to change.

The second reality Teresa welcomed in joy was this: she was loved and forgiven. She lived in a sea of mercy. This led Teresa to accept life rooted in her helpless sinfulness wrapped in the loving mercy of God. She was the creature caught in sin but a loved and forgiven child of God. God was the creator revealing his power in love and mercy. This truth of God's mercy is the foundation of three chapters in the second half of this book.

SELF-KNOWLEDGE, PRAYER, AND LIFE

Teresa of Ávila was relentless in declaring the importance of self-knowledge for the spiritual journey, the journey to God in the center of our being.

> Well now, it is foolish to think that we will enter heaven without entering ourselves, reflecting on our

misery and what we owe God and begging Him often
for mercy. * *THE INTERIOR CASTLE,* 2.1.11

For Teresa, prayer was the answer to almost all problems.
However, she had an expansive notion of prayer. It took
place in the context of the relationship between God at the
center and our life experience. In the interaction of these elements in prayer, self-knowledge has a pivotal role. The mystery of God unfolds in the dynamic of the person's prayer
and life experience. Self-understanding brings this process
together. When we accept the reality of God's place and our
place, God's mercy is the dominant issue. As she grew in
self-knowledge, Teresa grew steadily stronger in her oft-re-
peated conviction: "My life is the story of God's mercy."

As we grow in self-knowledge, we will celebrate our lives
as immersed in the sea of God's mercy. Self-knowledge will
gradually bring us to embrace the wonder of this gift.

There is no better way to understand and enter into this
relationship between God and ourselves than opening our
hearts to Jesus and his call. This is the theme of our next
chapter.

five

KEEPING OUR EYES FIXED ON JESUS

THE GOSPEL REVEALS TO US THE BASIS OF ALL CHRISTIAN SPIRITUALITY—WALKING WITH JESUS. It teaches us that to be a disciple of Jesus is to follow him. This is what Christian life is. Jesus basically demanded that we accept him as the way. The measure of our embracing the gospel is our response to this call.

The rich young man is one of the truly tragic figures in the gospels. He was the only one to reject Jesus' personal call. "Jesus looked steadily at him and loved him...he went away sad for he was a man of great wealth" (Mark 10:21–22). His wealth might be considered third-world poverty today. In a few decades he would lose everything with the invasion of the Romans. In contrast to the rich man's clear rejection, the disciples continued their journey with Jesus. They were filled with broken dreams, confusion, and fear, but in the end, they were faithful. They were learning that the heart is a battlefield of good and evil. Likewise, they experienced the heart creating idols which distorted reality. It also blinded and hardened the spirit.

In their struggle to understand Jesus, the disciples began to recognize the human dilemma of the fragmented heart. They were living what Paul articulated a few decades later in Romans: "We know that the law is spiritual, but I am carnal, sold into slavery to sin. What I do, I do not understand. For I do not do what I want, but I do what I hate" (Romans 7:14–15).

The second half of the Gospel of Mark portrays the disciples as a group on the edge of disillusionment. They are dealing with the frightening call to walk with Jesus to Jerusalem and the absolute shattering of their dreams and ambitions.

All the while Jesus continues calling them into the light, proclaiming the truth and preparing them to be free of the bondage of their self-absorption. The war in their fragmented hearts raged on. They were struggling with new self-knowledge that shattered their illusion of seeing Jesus as their ticket to power, wealth, and privilege.

After their rejection and abandonment of Jesus on that fatal weekend, they still clung together in bewilderment and at the edge of despair. With seemingly three years wasted, they feared they would be the next victims of the religious leaders. In the midst of this desperation and horror, Jesus appears with the incredibly merciful pronouncement, "Peace be with you" (John 20:21). There was no finger pointing, only unconditional acceptance and encouragement. Now it was a new day. With this last piece of the puzzle, the resurrection, in their hands, their job was to resolve the mystery of Jesus in their lives. This experience of God's mercy renewed their commitment. They were ready to shed the uncertainty and fright and walk with Jesus in spite of the continuing ambiguity of life.

MOVING FROM RELIGION TO SPIRITUALITY

The disciples are a good mirror for us. We share their uncertainty and anxiety amid our illusions that move us to seek happiness and security in the wrong places. We too suffer the consequences of a fragmented heart. We try to get by with the minimum for God and the maximum for ourselves. However, emptiness tends to surface eventually, deep in our being. The "dos and don'ts" of our religion no longer are enough. The question of the rich young man is rooted in the inevitable pull of the heart for something more.

This is where we move from our comfortable and safe approach to God in our religious rituals and practices to a search for something more profound. Spirituality is the whole process of growth from inauthenticity into full relationship with God and the possession of one's truth in the image of God. Spirituality draws us into the struggle where we move away from the shallow and illusionary to a more genuine relationship with God. This is a move from the formality of religion to a deeper spiritual path.

Despite our progress, we will eventually face the challenge of compromise. This is the ego's desperate maneuver to maintain control. We seek a space between the demands of the gospel and the comfort of the world. We subtly create our own gospel and make Jesus over in our image. As with Peter after his triple rejection, Jesus does not give up on us. He is always calling us to life. Each crisis manifests a deeper insight into the depth of our weakness and the grandeur of God's merciful love revealed in Christ crucified and Christ risen.

When Jesus calls, we need faith to accept him and join the journey. This demands a change in heart and mind that plays out in a series of conversions that slowly but steadily move away from compromise. The first leads us to communion with Jesus. The second points out that commitment to Jesus demands priority over everything else, even our own life. Finally, we are called, in conversion, into the paschal mystery of Christ crucified and Christ risen.

It is right at this juncture that the genius of St. Teresa of Ávila can be a great help. She is called the mother of spirituality. She offers us the challenge of addressing a few fundamental steps to grasp the call of personal authenticity that is central to any spirituality. First, we need to grow in self-knowledge that leads to humility. We then accept the consequences of this emerging insight: the interplay of our personal limits and the mercy of God. This is all done in prayer, which she describes as a conversation with someone we know loves us. Keeping our eyes fixed on Jesus nurtures this development. This is the story of the disciples. This is our story if we are open to the call.

For Teresa, it is the personal encounter in following Jesus that unveils the loving mercy of God. This gift has its privileged communication in prayer. Prayer is always her top priority. The prayerful encounter with Jesus constantly stands at the center of our pursuit of God, the final desire of the human heart.

"WHO DO YOU SAY THAT I AM?"

Few lessons of the gospel are more important than to keep our eyes fixed on Jesus. Walking with Jesus goes beyond the teachings of the church, beyond reading the Bible, beyond any devotions or other favorite religious expressions. Following Jesus is at the heart of faithful spirituality. Following Jesus turns our lives upside down. Following Jesus is the same today as it was in the day of the disciples. It calls us out of comfortable hiding places and takes us "where you do not want to go" (John 21:18).

The gospels are structured so that we, like Peter and the rest, meet Jesus in the wonders of his ministry. We are called to witness his teachings and healings. We are challenged to respond to his radical message of forgiveness and inclusion. We are invited to ponder the wonder of his compassion. We are asked to enter the stories. It helps to see ourselves as the person who gains sight, the leper who is cleansed, and the paralytic who is forgiven and healed.

In this way, like the disciples, we are led to the critical question: "Who do you say that I am?" (Mark 8:29). There is no question more imperative in our life. Who is Jesus for us?

For the disciples and for us, the consequences come slowly. We are on the road, but our encounter with Jesus is always partial and incomplete. Our relationship with Jesus always comes at a price, and a price that continues to escalate. At the heart of the encounter with Jesus is a transition—moving from our vision for happiness, from our priorities, to the new world of Jesus' vision and call. This conversion process repeats itself as we stay faithful with Jesus on the road to Jerusalem. Prayer leads to an ever-expanding awareness of God's will. A new and deeper experience of prayer flowing from these conversions empowers us to live in a way that is progressively guided by God's will. Eventually it calls us to say no to all that is not God. Our weakness is exposed dramatically. This struggle gradually reveals that the story of our life is the story of God's mercy.

The message of this book is the importance of prayer in following Jesus. In the next chapter we will consider what happens when our prayer matures in depth and consistency.

Six

WHAT HAPPENS WITHIN US WHEN WE PRAY REGULARLY?

PRAYER COMES AT A PRICE

WHEN WE PRAY REGULARLY THERE IS SERIOUS CHANGE IN OUR HEART. God's love is unrelenting in seeking more from us. This is why we come up with so many reasons we cannot pray. At the top of the list is *time* in one way or another: need to work, need to relax, need to be present to loved ones, need to...also watch TV, football, shopping, politics, etc. There are other reasons, such as being just too tired or sick and having too many heavy responsibilities. It all comes down to a question of determining what is important for us.

To this point, we have laid out the map for prayer. This has included the description and definition of prayer and two methods. Then we delved into the significance of the Bible, followed by the central role of self-knowledge. This led to the placement of Jesus' dominant presence in any authentic prayer life. As we now consider the benefits of these central elements of our prayer life, we need to remember that none of it will happen without the discipline of making prayer take place in our busy schedule.

Since God is so insistent, regular prayer will always bring us to the challenge of changing our lives. Prayer points out what God wants in a way that confronts our blind spots. The nature of deep personal prayer is to draw us out of comfortable deceptions. Examples of these deceptions are our inability to listen to others, our assumption of privilege and prestige, the power and depth of our prejudices, and many more. The journey to the center and its encounter with our loving God in prayer is not cost-free. The issue of time and the other excuses hindering our prayer are rooted in a fear of moving away from our comfort zone.

PRAYER BRINGS CHANGE

Here are a few examples of this inward transformation that happens when we are generous with our time for prayer. Many families are caught in the trap of a destructively addicted member. Everyone suffers. Al-Anon offers relief, but it comes with the demanding effort of self-knowledge. One needs to lose the illusion of control that thinks one can alter the person's behavior. It also confronts the patterns of denial or being a victim. Simply accepting that one cannot change another person comes slowly and with personal sacrifice. The change in attitude, however, is life-giving. This is the sort of thing that God is always surfacing in our prayer: movement from death to life, from illusion to reality. It is an invitation to accept the gospel values going beyond the superficial to reality.

In the early 1980s, already a priest for twenty years, I was challenged about my blatant prejudice against homosexuals. I fought it. I rejected it. I became angry. But I prayed. Eventually I began a journey to acceptance and repentance.

What is common in both of these issues, one personal and the other social or cultural, is that often in prayer a matter is brought to our awareness, but we resist it. However, it is now in play in our consciousness. If we pray regularly, we have to work hard to avoid it. The change evolving from our "hearing and obeying" in prayer sometimes is a matter of days or often months or even years. God is patient but never stops calling us out of the darkness to the light.

The "hear and obey" of Merton's definition of prayer is the encounter of our being with God's word and will. This means personal transformation when we are open and accepting of God's call. The message of the gospel is sown in our heart. These seeds of new life are always looking for good soil and the opportunity to blossom.

This is the goal of prayer: to slowly but surely create a new heart in the image of Jesus Christ. It is a gradual passage from self-absorption to self-giving.

PRAYER AS ACCEPTANCE

Teresa of Ávila's map of the spiritual journey is quite clear. It is an unyielding movement to the center, where God dwells. Prayer leads to a growing awareness of God calling us out of our selfishness to the loving presence that is our deepest truth. Prayer is the gateway for this self-discovery.

For Teresa, the "practice of prayer" was the serious pursuit of God. This involves all our life. Teresa's deliverance from mediocrity was the simple acceptance of reality. This acceptance involved herself, her world, and God. This led her to highlight the importance of humility, detachment, and charity. These three virtues were fundamental to her program.[3]

Humility was the acceptance of self as totally dependent on God. True self-knowledge leading to humility led her to accept both God's love and her human limitations. Detachment was the ability to see things clearly. Her possessions either brought her closer to God, or they were a roadblock on this journey. Charity was the ability to see and love others as God sees and loves them.

3　Teresa's program will be considered in more depth in the second part of this book in chapter twelve.

Her movement was from self-importance to humility. Attachments were her distorted use of things that then fragmented her heart. Some of these were seemingly innocent, some more destructive. All were obstacles to a commitment to prayer. At the top of the list of impediments to her quest for God in prayer was a heart rejecting both reconciliation and the needs of her brothers and sisters.

These three elements of humility, detachment, and love of neighbor were the foundation and context of the "practice of prayer" for Teresa that led her to be a mystic and doctor of the church.

In the end, our commitment to praying daily will lead us to an acceptance of life through humility, detachment, and love of neighbor. The discipline of finding a time and place to make prayer a non-negotiable part of our daily life will make us more comfortable accepting our brokenness in humility. The consequence of this regular conversation with someone who we know loves us will guide us in putting things in a perspective that is freeing rather than enslaving. The pilgrimage of self-discovery will lead us to see our service and love of neighbor as the continuing encounter with the God of love at our center.

When we do not achieve the balance of putting things in order, which is often the case, we encounter a human heart that has given way to the false gods. This is the "Enslaved Heart" that we ponder in the following chapter.

Seven

THE ENSLAVED HEART

THE WORSHIP OF FALSE GODS

ELIJAH HAD AN EPIC BATTLE ON MOUNT CARMEL WITH THE FALSE PROPHETS OF JEZEBEL, the patroness of the false god, Baal. Elijah, in the heat of the conflict, addressed the people with a question for all ages: "How long will you straddle the issue? If the Lord is God, follow him; if Baal, follow him" (1 Kings 18:21).

It seems like an easy choice for us. However, when Baal comes in the form of money, a more comfortable lifestyle, our bigotries, and especially our addictions, big and small, the choice becomes a great deal more clouded.

The human heart easily distorts our relationships with people, things, and ideas. There is a natural pull of compulsion. This relationship then gradually becomes an attachment for us. This is the foundational distortion. Basically, we are binding the human spirit to something or someone other than love. We are seeking God in the creature rather than letting the creature bring us to God. This is a major obstacle to our quest for God which is the foundation of any authentic spiritual life.

These attachments make life easier at first, but gradually we slide from the freedom of love to the fear of loss. Many attachments deteriorate into addictions, which further cut into our freedom in an escalating degree of compulsion. John of the Cross lists some very simple things that can be an attachment on the way to addiction: the habit of being excessively talkative, the way food is prepared, a book or a cell. Then, of course, there are personal relationships with the great capacity for distortion. In our consumer society, companies are spending gross amounts of money to enslave us to their products. The ever-expanding horizons of the digital world offer countless new opportunities for addiction.

LOSS OF FREEDOM
Every human being has addictions, almost always hidden in the safety of false consciousness. Addictions must be addressed to free our heart for God. The choice is simple

according to Elijah: "If the Lord is God, follow him; if Baal, follow him."

Addiction is a deeply disruptive process in the spiritual journey. It is a powerful and compulsive falsehood that stifles human freedom. It is basically an enslaving commitment, often under the guise of an innocent activity. Addictions run the gauntlet from deeply destructive behaviors, such as the abuse of alcohol and drugs, to seemingly innocuous activities like following your favorite team or family gossip. All addictions share one destructive element: reduction of the human freedom that is necessary in our search for God.

While the choice is simple, the identification of the dominating and freedom-robbing addictions is often quite complicated. It often takes years to expose our idols wrapped up in our ostensibly harmless addictions. The complexity of the twelve-step programs is a testimony to this challenge. Faithfulness to deep, personal prayer that leads to self-knowledge holds the key to overcoming addictions.

We long to settle down with the lesser gods who are lesser because we can control them. Among these lesser gods, our attachments and addictions hold the position of prominence. The heart struggles constantly with this excessive baggage that hinders the journey.

Addictions distort our most honest and real desire for truth and goodness: the basic hunger for God in our heart. Therefore, there is no such thing as a harmless addiction. All addictions are serious roadblocks on the journey to God.

The human heart is indeed an idol-making machine because of the basic reality of our addictions. The idols, the false gods we create so readily, produce disintegration and fragmentation within the heart. Freedom is the casualty. Often, we think of the idols of the Old Testament as foreign and unrelated to our experience. Yet what the idols expose is a fundamental and universal human experience. In *The Joy of the Gospel*, Pope Francis says the golden calf of our day is money and the market.

In prayer, God quite often raises the "addiction of the day" to consciousness. We see it clearly. We realize it calls for action. Most often we respond, "Not today, I gave at the office" or some other expression of evasion. No matter how strong our evasion, God is patient.

In these encounters in prayer, God offers quite doable options. Seldom does the truly big one, "the elephant in the room," enter our consciousness until we have made much progress with the more manageable addictions. The truly destructive addictions most often need the help of other individuals, and often of professionals and extended programs, to begin the healing process.

The purest acts of faith often come from the darkness of our addictions. Our helplessness sets us free from the illusion of being in charge. Our acts of faith and surrender seem to always be calling us into a risk. This letting go in faith seldom brings a sense of serenity and peace but instead an uncertainty that calls us to a naked and deeper trust in God.

When we are moving away from addictions, we are closer to Jesus in the Garden than Jesus in the transfiguration.

THE PILGRIMAGE

We regularly manufacture idols in a quest for security and control. On this point the Bible is clear, from Abraham to Jesus. A common theme of freedom in both the Hebrew Bible and the New Testament is the journey, the pilgrimage. Pilgrimage is the scriptural norm, and with it comes a basic insecurity and a call for trust and openness in life. We are driven by a distorted heart that wants security on our terms. We long for a stable home rather than the challenge of the uncertainty of the journey. We want to settle down with clear fences to define the limits of our reality. We gladly accept a mortgage to remove any semblance of uncertainty. To be king or queen of our own mansion goes much deeper than we think.

We enter the relentless battle of choosing good or evil, a false security or openness to God's call. Christ's parable of the weeds and the wheat (Matthew 13:24–30) symbolizes this ever-raging battle of grace and sin.

When we enter conflict with a strong addiction, the story of the Chosen People's sojourn in the desert is an excellent model of the inner turmoil. We seem lost and without direction. We are stripped down to the minimal elements of manna, quail, and water.

In the process of the purification, we learn more clearly than ever of both our sinfulness and our dependence on

God. The truth of the matter is raw, naked, and clear. We are the creature, sinful, broken, but loved and forgiven. God is the Creator, loving and merciful. The desert of the struggle to overcome addiction makes this clearer than ever.

THE CALL OF LOVE

When we get out of bed in the morning, we usually have a set of relationships and responsibilities that define our world. The call of the gospel demands a response of love and generosity in our concrete and specific world of family, work, community, and new expanding possibilities. However, the pull of the fragmented heart moves us to selfishness, neglect, and the narrowing routine of compulsion. The easy and closed world we have created for ourselves in the false security of our addictions protects our control and limits our horizons. Our mortgage needs to give way to the pilgrimage, to the freedom of the gospel's call.

The challenge of the gospel as seen through the tradition of Carmelite spirituality sets love as the priority. Love urges us to confront our small, controlled world and lifestyle. This means being open to others, starting with our immediate responsibilities and relationships and expanding to the appeal of our neighbor. This invitation is experienced on a personal level and on a social level. Both dimensions call us to be responsible for our world. Love pushes us toward the pilgrimage; the selfishness of the mortgage holds us back.

The idols of our time are not just personal loves and possessions but especially idols of power, prestige, control, exclusiveness, and dominance. These idols lead to neglect in our immediate relationships. They often blind us to the poor and their plight in our world, along with other issues of justice in society.

Our yearning for control resists the Lord's call to pilgrimage and trust. We face a fundamental choice just as in the time of Elijah or in today's message of Jesus: the true God or the god of our control, comfort, and convenience; the pilgrimage or the mortgage. It is almost always a choice of freedom or addiction.

Deep personal prayer draws us into a world of complexity and conflict on our way to peace. There are many complications in our prayer and the pursuit of God. The next chapter will delve into these matters.

Eight

DIFFICULTIES IN PRAYER

THE BASIC REASON FOR DIFFICULTIES IN PRAYER IS THAT GOD IS A JEALOUS LOVER WITH LITTLE PATIENCE FOR RIVALS. There is no limit to his love for us. God is always calling us to surrender, to accept this love, to be singular in our commitment. There is a price we have to pay for this encounter. It is the death of our selfishness; our ego has to lessen its role of supremacy. This is the basis for our difficulties in prayer. This battle takes place in the perennial conflict of finding time for prayer. If we have a child in critical condition in the hospital or, on a more mundane level, if our favorite team is playing in the finals of the World Cup or the

Super Bowl, time is not an issue. We find time for what is important to us.

Teresa of Ávila tells us prayer is a conversation with someone who we know loves us. Our difficulty is overcoming our self-love to let our love of God rise to the top of our agenda. To do this, we face the challenge of change, often deep personal change. Teresa says that prayer and comfortable living are not compatible. Prayer demands sacrifice that claims our time and then our lifestyle. This is why prayer presents us with an ongoing challenge.

When we are praying, distractions are the immediate obstruction. The direct answer is to regain our focus. This is done by returning to the text or our prayer word, the mantra. This is all part of the battle of prayer. The ego insists on being in charge. The Spirit is calling us to let go. We need confidence, acceptance, and surrender to God.

The root of distractions is this conflict of the ego and the Spirit. The distractions will not go away completely until God takes over within us in intense contemplative prayer. In the meanwhile, we need to understand there is gold to be found in the struggle against our relentless flights of fancy that are our distractions.

On the conscious level, our struggle is between our ego's unending quests for control and our gradual submission to God. At a deeper level, God often uses distractions to surface issues and concerns that help us on the road to self-knowledge and humility. Frequently, what seems like a total waste of time is, in fact, a beautiful invitation to embrace humility. There may be a hidden fear that surfaces as a distraction. It may be a troubled relationship we are avoiding. The ever-present addictions always are part of the program of distractions. Whatever the distractions, we should pay attention to them in reflection outside of prayer. They often hold nuggets of gold for true self-knowledge.

THE TRUE CENTER

Thomas Merton brought the concept of centering into the modern understanding of prayer. This idea is based on the insight that God is the deepest truth about each human being. God is at the center. Our true self is to live at this center in total faithfulness.

This concept of the true self flows from Jesus' declaration that one who seeks to save his life will lose it, and the one who loses his life for Christ's sake will save it (Matthew 10:39; Luke 9:24; Mark 8:35). Our understanding of this teaching refers to the spiritual struggle we all encounter between the false self and the true self.

The true self is who I am in God. It is the core of myself free of all blindness that comes from our broken human condition. To live out of the true self is the goal of the purification and transformation that is the conclusion of a demanding and faithful pilgrimage. This leads to reception of God in our life.

This passage to the center means moving beyond our superficial self, the self that is enthralled by the false values of a consumer society. This is the self that creates a false center of self-absorption. This is the self that lives with the illusion of grandiosity. This false self exaggerates the importance of appearances and perceptions. This is the self that is dominated by the ego to create a world centered on oneself. This is the destructive pattern of selfishness that we must eliminate.

Prayer is basically creating a path of change that reduces the false self and opens the path to the true self. This is centering. This is the call to a contemplative approach to life. The difficulties in prayer are rooted in this surrender, which creates the movement to the true self. The journey in prayer is almost always limited and deficient. It is a great help for us to have a clear grasp of where we are going: to the center where the true self is one with God. Therefore, we can see that the content of the early chapters relates to the prayer journey. It is all a piece drawing us into the Mystery of Love revealed by Jesus.

True spiritual maturity is complete human development. This is our goal. It is not a withdrawal from life but the utmost acceptance of life with God at the center. We need to move away from the passion to control our possessions and relationships. We need to possess them in freedom and be open to self-giving service. This is the purpose of the gospel journey of walking with Jesus.

TERESA AND PRAYER
Love for our brothers and sisters is the unyielding message of Jesus. From the Our Father to the mystical heights of

John's Last Supper, the message is clear and forceful: "love one another as I have loved you" (John 15:12). The ultimate challenge to the journey with Jesus is the call to love our neighbor. Likewise, there is no more overriding impediment in our journey to the center than our failure to love one another.

We all have stories of personal mistreatment, neglect, betrayal, and even violence done to us. We create tapes in our mind and imagination of these personal indignities. These tapes often dominate our time at prayer.

In another area, our inordinate attachments and all manner of lesser attachments are another source for the false self to penetrate our prayer time. Both the personal hurts and our attachments prop up the false self's war against our focus in prayer. It is an issue of life or death for the false self. Interior peace and order are the death knell for the ego's control.

I repeat again, the human heart is an idol-making machine. These idols try to make the good things of God's creation into a more comfortable and convenient god under our control and often in our image. This totally short-circuits the journey to the center.

Humility, detachment, and love for one another are powerful antidotes to the upheaval caused by our idols, distractions, and personal hurts during prayer. They create a peace and right order within us. They facilitate the journey to the center that will eventually overcome our difficulties in prayer. Humility, detachment, and love for our sisters and brothers attack the chaos coming from self-importance, attachments, addictions, and personal and social animosity. We need to move away from the clutching and clinging to these idols in our effort to control our possessions and relationships. These virtues help us to use our possessions to encourage life, not distort it.

These three virtues create harmony and a sense of transparency in our prayer life. We grow in the healthy relationship to ourselves, to others, and to God. The result is an interior stillness that is a great help to prayer. Distractions are not eliminated, but they are reduced and their intensity lessened.

We have seen the importance of self-knowledge, the Bible, the centrality of Jesus' role, along with how the positive changes of prayer and the negative pull of an enslaved heart affect our prayer journey. In the final chapter of this first half of our text we will see how these elements are incarnated in our life experience, the first and primary source of our experience of God.

Nine

LIFE IS THE GREATEST GRACE

THOMAS MERTON MADE MANY CONTRIBUTIONS TO THE EVOLVING SPIRITUALITY IN OUR DAY. He brought contemplation as a goal for all Christians out of the dark ages that had seen it as the privilege of a few. Likewise, he presented contemplative spirituality as a desirable option for every serious Christian.

Using a traditional theological fact that God is everywhere, he pointed out that God is the ground of our being. We cannot exist outside of God. Merton showed how this truth invites us into a contemplative spirituality that starts with the reality that God is not only within us, but that our most authentic self is embedded in that presence. Contemplation gives us clarity in awareness of what already is. We are united to God. We are already one. Our task is to overcome the consequences of sin by the purification and transformation of contemplation in order to live this new oneness. What Merton identified as the Hidden Ground of Love is the starting point in our spiritual journey.

In March 1958, Thomas Merton had been a Trappist monk for eighteen years and a famous author for a good part of that time. He was on his way to becoming a major international spiritual force in the twentieth century. On March 18, he left his monastery to go to the nearby city of Louisville to get some printing done. Amid the large crowd of shoppers on the street, he had a special experience. In describing this experience Merton said,

> In Louisville, at the corner of Fourth and Walnut, in the center of the shopping district, I was suddenly overwhelmed with the realization that I loved all those people, that they were mine and I theirs, that we could not be alien to one another even though we were total strangers....The sense of liberation from the illusory difference was such a relief and such a joy to me that I almost laughed out loud...thank God, thank God that I am like other men, that I am only a man among others....Then it was as if I suddenly saw the secret beauty of their hearts, the depths of their hearts, where neither sin nor desire nor self-knowl-

edge can reach, the core of their being, the person that each one is in God's eyes. If only they could see themselves as they really are. If only we could see each other that way all the time. There would be no more war, no more hatred, no more greed.[4]

Through this special contemplative grace, a gift from God, Merton saw what God sees. This is the unity that pure love experiences when it is unhindered by the divisive consequences of the original sin. This is the goal for all of us. This is the call to paradise that leads to contemplation.

We all suffer from a distorted sense of spirituality that works against this fundamental unity. One feature of this deception sets up special places for God. Sunday Mass, the sacraments, retreats, and many other "distinct" times of prayer are perceived as sacred moments. When we enter a church we often say it is beautiful. Most often we mean it fits our sense of a sacred and special place that makes us feel closer to God.

Merton's insight into God as the ground of being was expressed in one of his many books, *The Hidden Ground of Love*.[5] All of life happens in this hidden ground of love. We are embedded in this presence of God to us. Therefore, all of

---

4 Thomas Merton, *Conjectures of a Guilty Bystander* (Garden City, NY: Image, 1968), pp.156-58.

5 Thomas Merton, *The Hidden Ground of Love* (New York: Farr Strauss Giroux, 1985).

life is sacred. The problem is that we divide and isolate our understanding of how God is present to us. There is a Zen saying that can help us here: *If we understand, things are as they are. If we do not understand, things are as they are.*

Life is where God is. This is why we can say that life is the greatest grace. The special moments of prayer and sacred space, the times set aside for the sacraments, retreat, and reflection, are truly important. They bring us to an awareness of what already is. Most often, however, in the ordinary flow of things, we fail to realize we are in the presence of God.

We all have singular moments when God seems to be playing peek-a-boo with us. In these isolated events, we have our breath taken away with the grandeur and beauty of an event that bursts into our consciousness: falling in love, the birth of a child, a sunset, an awesome experience of the power of the oceans or celestial reality. Then there are much less frequent times when we have what are called unitive moments. Here the cover is removed and, at the deepest part of our being, we experience our oneness with all and with God. Contemplation produces an awareness of the presence of God that is growth in our normal consciousness in this movement to oneness. Merton's "Louisville experience" is an excellent example of this unitive experience.

Much of our spirituality is rooted in a distorted view that God is more here and less there and not at all in another place. The fact is that the foundation of any faithful and integrated spirituality must flow from Merton's insight that God is the ground of our being. All creatures exist because of this presence. The distortion is when we separate God from his creatures in our divided and isolated spirituality.

God is no less present at the kitchen table on Sunday afternoon than at the Mass on Sunday morning. God is just as present to the garbage collector serving the community or the struggling drug addict or a nun in her contemplative convent. For each of these individuals and for us, the primary issue is our awareness of God's presence. An integrated spirituality will lead us to contemplative prayer. We need this kind of prayer to expand our awareness of the loving and saving presence of God in all of life. We use the sacred moments of prayer, retreats, sacraments, and just openness to life to grow in that awareness.

Prayer flows from the deepest human reality, God within us. In this hidden ground of love, God is always taking the initiative. God never stops beckoning us to the true life. Prayer is a secondary response to this invitation of God. Life is the first response. Our experience is only possible because of God's loving presence. Life is the greatest grace because of this divine bonding. Prayer opens us up to what already is our relationship to God calling us home. Prayer is the guiding light to God at our center. In this context, prayer helps us understand and respond to our initial experience of God in our lived reality.

While God is everywhere, we have only one option to experience that presence. It is in our life. Our task is to seek the faithfulness, integrity, and honesty to live with a growing awareness and commitment to God's presence. This is always a call to deeper life in the mystery of love. The initial encounter takes place within us. Then we move outward to our brothers and sisters. We slowly learn that all is grace. We are drawn away from separateness and division to the inclusiveness of Christ's message. Among the many stories of inclusiveness in the gospels, three marvelous examples are the good Samaritan, the woman at the well, and the healing of the lepers. They all celebrate the outcasts being invited into the community. Eventually, we open up to our responsibility to transform this world in accord with God's plan for the kingdom of justice and peace, where we build bridges not walls.

ALL LIFE FLOWS FROM GOD

In the context of this integrated spirituality we often say only God matters. This comes off as unreal and life-denying. It is not. We need to realize that all that is good, all that is beautiful and life-giving in our relationships, in our responsibilities, in the deepest love in our heart, are powerful and meaningful because they flow from God. Their goodness and beauty, so significant for us in our ordinary experience, reflects their rootedness in God. Watching children grow up or the peaceful death of a long-suffering parent or grandparent simply exposes the reality of God's presence. It is a little more remote with the celebration of the success of a child in school or a teen's first date. The fact is the total spectrum of our experiences emerges from the sacred presence of a loving and merciful God.

All experience of love in our life originates from God. This is where it gets its power to be real for us. Love remains the deepest of all human mysteries because it flows from the mystery of God. However, because we are sinful, most human encounters with love are limited and deficient. The gospel journey with Jesus is our invitation to the purifying and transforming process to make this love continually more selfless. Deep personal prayer helps us more than anything else in this journey with Jesus.

In this chapter we gained a much richer insight into a most important theme: the constant connection between prayer and life.

SECTION TWO

Contemplation

Ten

THE MOVE TO CONTEMPLATION

In the second part of this book on deep personal prayer, we are going to consider Teresa of Ávila's call to the Contemplative Switch. In her classic on the spiritual life, *The Interior Castle*, Teresa lays out a clear and beautiful description of the spiritual journey, the way we grow in awareness of our experience of God. She sees seven levels or dwelling places on the way to the center, where we have the full encounter with God in union.

The human heart was made for God. All of life reveals movements of various intensity where the heart is responding to its fundamental hunger. These experiences expose a journey to the center where God resides. *The Interior Castle* lays out these seven different steps, called dwelling places. The seventh dwelling places describes life in and from the center. This is the complete fulfillment of the human heart in union with God. The first three dwelling places are the beginnings. These describe first steps of the journey. The fourth, fifth, and sixth dwelling places are rooted in contemplation that engenders a profound purification and transformation of the person. The conclusion of the journey is in the full human development of the person and union with God in the seventh dwelling places.

The basic structure of *The Interior Castle* illustrates the seven dwelling places and how each dwelling place identifies progress toward the center. The soul moves from room to room as it advances in the spiritual life. For the most part, none of the dwelling places offers a quick and easy passage to the next dwelling places. Our experience is more fluid, much more of a push and pull, a give and take in the process of movement toward total union with God at the center of the seventh dwelling places. The first three dwelling places show the beginning phases concluding in the most fascinating stage for pastoral ministry, the third dwelling places.

In the first two dwelling places, there is an initial encounter with the transcendent. This leads to a moral struggle to activate the conversion process. In the third dwelling places, we experience relief from the consuming moral struggle of the second dwelling places. There is a sense of having arrived at a very good place. We have a clear perception of progress against the forces of evil. Yet, the conflict of good and evil is never far from the surface.

The great temptation of the third dwelling places is a false sense of having arrived. Prevalent to a degree in each of the dwelling places, this self-deception dominates in the third dwelling places. The central issue is to move on to the Contemplative Switch.

In the fourth dwelling places, there is a new and different experience of God. This is both the beginning of contemplation and a bridge to the deeper purifying and transforming experience of God in the fifth and sixth dwelling places.

Finally, in the seventh dwelling places, the journey reaches the goal of union with God.

As we search for a clearer understanding of the prayer journey, the critical part for us to grasp is the Contemplative Switch. This is the passage from the third to the fourth dwelling places. This is the beginning of contemplation, which is a new and totally different presence and experience of God. There is a firsthand loving knowledge and presence that accomplishes change we could never do on our own. This is where we hope to arrive by our faithful dedication to deep personal prayer.

In this section, there are four chapters. We will consider the Contemplative Switch in detail. Then we will look at three aspects of Teresa's teachings that are a general support for anyone who is serious about the deep personal prayer to prepare them for the gift of contemplation. Teresa's program, her special bookmark prayer, and her call to "get real" are approaches and experiences that are especially helpful in preparing one for the gift of contemplation.

Contemplation does not happen unless there is significant surrender on our part. The Contemplative Switch occurs when we experience a deep sense of being loved by God. This helps us accept ourselves in both our brokenness and giftedness. Now our prayer is that God will set us free to love with a pure heart.

Teresa's fundamental insight is worthy of repeating again. She saw her relation to God as fundamental to all. God is the Creator, kind, merciful, and loving, calling us into the mystery of love and mercy. She was the creature: sinful but loved and forgiven, called to surrender into the mystery of love and mercy.

All of this was taking place in the reality of her personal experience. She understood well that life is the greatest grace. Therefore, the following are central to her message:

1. Self-knowledge allowed her to see herself in relation to God as the Creator and moved her away from the distortion of seeing herself as the center.

2. She saw life as the great grace because it is pregnant with the possibility of new love and freedom as one moves to the true center.

3. She understood the need to accept reality as it is and not as she wished to impose her will on it. In

accepting reality, she was open to the pull of God's call no matter how it seemed contrary to her plans and interests.

4. She saw her problems and difficulties as possible sources of freedom in her pursuit of God, even though they appeared in conflict with her immediate goals and desires.

5. She learned to interpret reality by the measure of how it brought her closer to God and not as a source of her comfort, prestige, and power. This is what she meant by "get real."

6. For Teresa, prayer is the singular gift that helped her see and embrace God calling her into the mystery. Prayer is a means to an end: finding and loving God in our life experience.

7. Teresa's program of humility, detachment, and love for our brothers and sisters is the source to overcome the inner turmoil and disorder, the consequences of sin within us. This inner chaos is the dominant obstacle to prayer. For her, failure to pray with depth and regularity short-circuited the entire quest to enter into the mystery of love and mercy, which is the calling of all humanity.

Eleven

THE CONTEMPLATIVE SWITCH
Moving On Up or Else

As we found out in Chapter Ten, the Introduction to Section Two, Teresa of Ávila lays out a map for seeking God in her classic on the spiritual life, *The Interior Castle*. She describes seven stages or dwelling places. For most of us, the third dwelling places is most relevant to our search.

The movement from the third dwelling places to the fourth dwelling places in *The Interior Castle* seems irrelevant to our life today. The reality, however, is different. The stagnation in the third dwelling places is the reason we have so much bickering within Christian groups and among loved ones. It is the source of so much tension in staff meetings and at the dinner table. It is the basis of many of our problems in personal relations and the division between groups.

The Contemplative Switch, this movement from the third dwelling places to the fourth dwelling places, occurs when we enter a new dimension of God's love for us. It becomes intensely personal. This helps us accept ourselves as we are, flawed and incomplete, graced and blessed. We begin to wait and listen to God. We are more open to be taught by God, more receptive to God in life. The desire to control God continues to lessen. We long for a pure heart. This is the yearning for contemplation.

In describing this path, Teresa offers us a profoundly pastoral and practical message. Her teachings open great vistas of possible new understanding and reconciliation.

The Contemplative Switch, moving to the fourth dwelling places and the beginning of contemplation, is based on these fundamental teachings of Teresa:

1. Having arrived in the third dwelling places, the person is in a good place because of a meaningful moral conversion.

2. The strain at this point in the spiritual journey contrasts God's call to move on and the person's desire to settle down and enjoy the progress.

3. The great difficulty is that the flagrant egoism of the previous dwelling places has gone underground. Now it surfaces in the cloak of virtue that feeds one's self-righteousness and hypocrisy in a way that is destructive and divisive at all levels.

4. This newly hidden selfishness is the dominant obstacle to progress. "To let go and let God" is a long, arduous passage. Teresa wavered around this decision for almost two decades in spite of a faithful prayer life.

Teresa's teaching on the Contemplative Switch points to three possibilities:

1. rejection of God's call, which leads to division, hostility, and conflict;

2. faithfulness to the struggle to move ahead, which opens possibilities of growth and reconciliation;

3. surrender to God's call, leading to the seeds of peace, harmony, and justice in contemplation.

In his personal testimonial, *The Joy of the Gospel*, Pope Francis gives a vivid description of this failure to "move on up," forsaking the battle to go beyond the third dwelling places:

> Those who have fallen into this worldliness look on from above and afar, they reject the prophecy of their brothers and sisters, they discredit those who raise questions, they constantly point out the mistakes of others and they are obsessed by appearances....This is a tremendous corruption disguised as a good. We need to avoid it by making the Church constantly go out from herself, keeping her mission focused on Jesus Christ, and her commitment to the poor. God save us from a worldly Church with superficial spiritual and pastoral trappings. This stifling worldliness can only be healed by breathing in the pure air of the Holy Spirit who frees us from self-centeredness cloaked in an outward religiosity bereft of God.
>
> ❋ N. 97

Here are a few concrete examples from parish life of the ego operating in the name of virtue that wreak havoc and division. The same reality of the hidden ego at work is operative in family life, at work, and in the larger community.

- a eucharistic minister who insists on distributing the "bread" and not the "cup";

- an ethnic group celebrating the unity and love of the Eucharist while intensely angry at another ethnic group of the parish selling used clothes outside during the Mass;

- a pastor who is deaf and blind when dealing with the recommendations of the parish council and finance committee;

- parents who are incapable of receiving any criticism of their child from a teacher;

- chronic blaming of "those people" for the dirty kitchen, even though they have no idea of who last used the facility.

These are just the firecrackers of parish life. The more destructive landmines of ethnic division and power struggles are examples of the many hurtful events constantly challenging unity. Among many forces driving the church away from gospel values are clericalism, the abuse of power by some bishops, and the Vatican bureaucracy's hunger to control. Pope Francis' call for a "revolution of tenderness" often seems a long way off.

Teresa has this powerful and relevant statement in this crisis of "moving on up" from the third dwelling places to the fourth dwelling places:

> With humility present, this state (third dwelling places) is a most excellent one. If humility is lacking, we will remain here our whole life and with a thousand afflictions and miseries. For since we will not have abandoned ourselves, this state will be very laborious and burdensome. We shall be walking while weighed down with this mud of our human misery, which is not so with those who ascend to the remaining rooms.
>
> ✻ *THE INTERIOR CASTLE*, **3.2.9**

THE CONTEMPLATIVE SWITCH

This teaching of Teresa is truly insightful. The gospels give us a marvelous vision into this struggle of the Contemplative Switch. The stories of the rich young man, Peter's rejection of Jesus, and the woman with the twelve-year hemorrhage help us understand the process.

Teresa always connects the third dwelling places to the rich young man. As the gospel states, "Jesus looked on him with love" (Mark 10:21). When pushed to choose, "he became sad because he had many possessions" (Matthew 19:22). (A fair description of his wealth in the time of Jesus would be two donkeys or a horse if he was truly rich, at least three sets of clothing, servants, land, and a fancy outhouse.) This incident is the only situation in all the gospels where an individual directly rejects Jesus' personal call.

Contrast that with the story of Peter's denials. "At that instant while he was still speaking, the cock crew, the Lord turned and looked straight at Peter...and he went out and wept bitterly" (Luke 22:60–62). Peter offers a beautiful picture of Teresa's teaching on humility: the truth of our total dependence on the mercy of God. This is a profound experience of redemption for Peter. He moves away from his self-righteousness and control: "Even though I have to die with you, I will never deny you" (Matthew 26:35). In his tears, he reveals his abandonment to the merciful embrace of a loving God. This is a giant step on the road to contemplation.

A third person who helps us to understand this Contemplative Switch is the woman plagued with her disease for twelve years. In saying, "If only I can touch his cloak, I will be cured" (Matthew 9:21), the woman saw in Jesus not just hope for her physical healing but the fulfillment of the deepest longing in her heart. Her eyes of faith let her see in Jesus the mystery of love made flesh. She saw in Jesus the completeness of liberation, redemption, and eternal life. This call to life begins now in this monumental encounter of love. Jesus said, "Courage, daughter, your faith has saved you" (Matthew 9:22). This miracle, like others, is a symbol of the purifying and transforming experience of the new presence of God in contemplation.

These are our choices in the third dwelling places. We can reject the call and hug our "donkey" for security. We can continue the struggle in humility facing our poverty. We can "let go and let God" by touching the mantle of his cloak to move on to the deeper life of contemplation. The key for all of us facing these enormous choices is a life of deep personal prayer, the foundation of a mature spiritual life. Teresa's program of humility, detachment, and love for the brothers and sisters is the great support in this grand venture. We have referred to this program three times in previous chapters. We will now elaborate a more thorough consideration of this fundamental insight of Teresa.

Twelve

TERESA'S PROGRAM
The Foundation of Prayer

WHEN WE BEGIN TO PRAY IN A DEEPER AND MORE COM-
MITTED WAY, it is almost always a response to a hunger in
our heart for something more. Generally, a moral conversion
has brought some sense of outward order in our life. Prayer
is a call to enter within to a richer, undiscovered world.

We have come to a point in life where we are fundamentally dissatisfied. We are willing to take the spiritual journey
more seriously. The movement inward leads to prayer. At
first, it is easy enough and comforting. However, the very

thrill of victory draws us into the agony of defeat. There is a price to pay. This leads us to the fundamental problem: ambivalence. We see the spiritual journey as important, but it has to work in the context of our clear personal commitments. We are not anxious to shatter our schedule, to give up too much time, change our priorities, and especially address our relationships, good and bad.

This is the heart of the problem. Behind the call to pilgrimage to God is a God who continually tests our generosity. We will slowly realize that the divine price tag goes beyond our wildest dreams. Prayer brings us face to face with the ambiguity of the human condition. Our heart is pulled in many directions: between the divine and mundane, between the body and the spirit, between transcendent and the transient, between surrender and control.

Faithful prayer eventually reveals the depth of our fragmented heart. These contradictions often hinder, and even consume, our prayer time. The tapes of our hurts play over and over in our mind. The pull of our attachments and the fear of change begin to make prayer a troublesome challenge. We all have our non-negotiables: the things we do not intend to change. God often surfaces these specific items in prayer, usually only one at a time. Often, we escape the confrontation in the comfort of our distractions.

There is need for order at a personal level. This comes slowly as we are faithful to prayer. Yet prayer needs the support of personal change in our life. This is where the program of Teresa fits in. She insists that humility, detachment, and charity are essential virtues throughout the prayer journey. They are its foundation.

The dilemma is that we need prayer to grow in humility, detachment, and charity. Our commitment to pray, then, is a dynamic relation between the virtues changing how we live and, in turn, how we pray to strengthen these very same virtues. There is a mutual growth cycle. It deepens both the prayer and the virtues on the way to the final goal of personal integration.

The three virtues lead us to an emerging sense of acceptance of all aspects of our life. This is the beginning of withdrawal from the trap of ambiguity that torments the human experience. This acceptance tends to bring order within our life. We begin to accept our reality in all its ambivalence, confusion, and brokenness. This acceptance, which is the source of humility, detachment, and charity, opens us to the call of love. It pulls us away from the lies of selfishness, misuse of God's creatures, and hostility to our sisters and brothers.

THE THREE VIRTUES

Humility is the truth. This virtue makes us aware of our total dependence on God as our Creator. We are the creatures, sinful and broken. Humility is the acceptance of this complete dependency on a loving and merciful God. As we grow deeper in prayer, there is slow revelation of the self that is consumed in every manner of self-importance. Humility helps us to accept this painful self-knowledge. As humility grows, we begin to see more clearly that all good things come from God.

Teresa is not talking about a loss of self-esteem, a false and destructive misrepresentation of humility. Such a state is disturbing and conflicted. Teresa, on the contrary, says, "Humility does not disturb or disquiet however great it may be; it comes with peace, delight, and calm...this humility expands the soul and enables it to serve God more" (*Way of Perfection*, 10.2).

Detachment is placing all God's creatures in the right order. It is a basic acceptance of ourselves. We gradually see the distortions of a fragmented heart that are constantly manufacturing false gods that put us at the center. These falsehoods magnify our sense of self-importance. The gift of detachment can free us from something as overwhelming as an addiction to drugs or alcohol. It also can help us leave a favorite TV show or football game to help someone. Detachment is a basic freedom from anything and everything that offers an obstacle to doing God's will.

For Teresa, detachment was the underlying subject when she frequently talked about poverty of spirit, mortification, and surrender to God's will. This brought her to see an intimate connection between humility and detachment.

In the past, there were many names used to describe detachment. Mortification, abnegation, and self-sacrifice were a few of them. Today the more acceptable terms are spiritual freedom and availability for apostolic work. Regardless of the terminology, the simple fact is we are set free from enslavement to any deterrents to embracing God's will.

Thomas Merton has this insight on the topic:

> Only the person who is free from attachment finds that creatures have become his friends. As long as he is attached to them, they speak to him only of his own desires...when he is selfish, they serve his selfishness. When he is free, they speak to him of God.[6]

Charity is the proper acceptance of others. As much as Teresa treasured prayer, she was insistent that love for our brothers and sisters determined our spiritual growth. For her, the inner journey is validated by the quality of our interpersonal relations. This love is the essential condition for movement toward the center, where God awaits. We are called to share in God's love for all.

This call for communal love is the most difficult obstacle on our pilgrimage to God. Our selfishness has incredible powers to twist things in justifying our judgmental self-righteousness. Teresa understood this well. She said,

> Beg our Lord to give you this perfect love of neighbor. Let his Majesty have a free hand, for He will give you more than you know how to desire because you are

---

6   Thomas Merton, *No Man Is an Island* (New York: Harcourt Brace, 1955), p. 9.

striving and making every effort to do what you can about this love, and force your will to do the will of your Sister in everything even though you lose your rights; forget your own good for their sakes no matter how much resistance your nature puts up; and, when the occasion arises, strive to accept work yourself so as to relieve your neighbor of it.

❋ *THE INTERIOR CASTLE,* 5.3.12

VIRTUES BRING ORDER

Teresa understood that the obstacles to prayer are rooted in the disorder in our relation to God, to God's creatures, and to our sisters and brothers. It is hard to pray when the heart is laden with personal hurts and disrespect for our dignity. When we bring the distortions of our addictions, great and small, to prayer, it is a painful task to center our heart on God. When our heart is consumed with animosity and anger, prayer happens with difficulty, if at all.

Humility, detachment, and charity bring a growing sense of order and peace. They produce an atmosphere open to the sacred. They nourish a freedom from all the divisions flowing from our fragmented heart. The virtues do not eliminate the problems in our life. They do, however, help us cope with them in a more serene and accepting way.

While inner peace is the goal, it is only achieved in spiritual warfare. The spiritual combat is relentless in its demands. The virtues are weak in the beginning but gradually grow with the help of prayer. Prayer seeks this growth to build up its staying power in the battle against inner turmoil. We are less troubled. The mayhem of life begins to decline. Something special is happening. There is a new and free self that evolves out of the dynamic. This personal transformation flows from a new relation to the self in humility, to our possessions in detachment, and to others in love. This is our goal until God intervenes and takes over in contemplation to finish the personal transformation.

Teresa's teaching on acceptance is best illustrated in her bookmark prayer. This is the topic of the next chapter. Acceptance of reality on God's terms is the product of a long spiritual journey. Teresa's prayer is a great guide on that journey to contemplation.

Thirteen

TERESA'S PRAYER
Call to Acceptance

"Be not afraid," or similar wording, appears as a Scripture verse over three hundred times in the Bible. It always reveals a sense of God's caring presence.

Teresa accepted this loving providence as the foundation of reality. It is the center of her message in her famous bookmark prayer. The prayer is an invitation into the mystery of God's loving presence. It invites us to accept life as it is. For Teresa, an honest openness to life draws us into God's love. Life is the greatest grace. Jesus revealed this power of acceptance when he prayed in the Garden, "Not my will, but thy will be done" (Luke 22:42).

May nothing disturb you.
May nothing make you afraid.
Everything passes.
God alone never changes.
Patience can attain anything.
He who has God within lacks nothing.
God is enough!

Letting go of the illusions of our control of reality is a dominant part of Teresa's teachings. Letting go and letting God in a surrender of accepting our life situation is a centerpiece of Teresa's message. This evolves from a persistent growth toward our spiritual maturity. Most of us have a long way to go. Acceptance is much more of a goal than a reality. We need to continue the struggle. We can only make our way one step at a time.

This acceptance does not make us robots. We have responsibility to live life to its full potential with integrity and authenticity. We do this by developing our talents, meeting our responsibilities, and enriching our relationships. We need to be attentive, intelligent, reasonable, responsible, and loving in all things. Soon enough we will run into the arbitrariness and dark side of reality beyond our control: sickness, inequality, prejudice, fractured relationships, and countless other dimensions of life. We just cannot cut and paste to resolve the problem. Slowly we learn that the difficulties of life are simply part of our common human experience. The issue is how we respond to these complications. This is the critical role of acceptance.

We all find ourselves somewhere on the journey. When the challenges escalate, our level of acceptance is often not up to the task. The beautiful prayer of Teresa vanishes into space in the storm of our anxieties and fears. Letting go of the illusion of our control of reality is the challenge of Teresa's prayer. We need a great deal of help to expand our heart for this task.

BEING IN CONTROL:
FROM THE BALLGAME TO LIFE

I remember a glorious moment when I was a youngster. It was 1949. The White Sox, my favorite baseball team, were on an extended winning streak. It marked an emergence from several decades of mediocrity. During this winning streak, I created a surefire way to help the team win. While I listened on the radio and they needed help, I knelt on the couch and stuffed my head into the corner of the couch.

My sisters told me I was crazy, but the Sox kept winning. Until they lost. My inability to help the White Sox was the beginning of a long and continuing passage. I was learning that I could not control reality. In accepting my failure to help the White Sox I slowly realized that the Yankees were a better team.

I have spent the rest of my life creating much more sophisticated methods of trying to control reality. All have been equally futile in the end. I suppose you would describe it as being strong-willed, closed-minded, ideological, and even an unrealistic dreamer. What these efforts had in common was a lack of acceptance, along with a passionate desire to make reality fit my terms. I think I share this practice with most people.

Teresa's prayer is an invitation to get real, to be open to life in all its brokenness and limits, as well as its beauty and wonder. This is where we encounter God, not in the illusions and deceptions of our self-centered heart seeking to control reality.

WILLINGNESS AND WILLFULNESS

Gerald May was a prominent psychiatrist who evolved into a prolific and excellent writer on spirituality. One of the many insights he has contributed to our modern understanding of spirituality is the paradox of willingness and willfulness. These concepts were first explained in *Will and Spirit*[7] but are found in all his subsequent writings.

Willingness means surrender to the deepest processes of life. We accept that we belong to a reality beyond our self. It has the sense of letting go of our separateness and sharing a new oneness with the Mystery that is the foundation of reality. It is a desire to participate in reality beyond the bounds of self and our control. In contrast, willfulness centers on self-mastery. It seeks to put the focus on controlling

---

7   Gerald May, *Will and Spirit* (San Francisco: Harper & Row, 1982).

and manipulating reality to preserve the attention and control on oneself.

Willingness is saying yes to a call into life beyond our control. Willfulness is not ready to cede the control. The best it can come up with is "yes, but…" Willingness and willfulness are expressions of a general attitude to life and its foundational mystery. However, we cannot use them to discern specific events and actions.

In Teresa's prayer, and in all her teachings, she celebrates willingness as the way to God. This is the way of acceptance. For her, acceptance is to forsake the relentless conflict of resisting God's call. Along with May, Teresa understands well the power of letting go. There is freedom flowing from acceptance. In the end, the journey to God is more about diminishment than acquisition. Our natural inclination is the opposite. We think all progress is made by creating power and domination. We long for the necessary tools to achieve these goals. In the spiritual way, on the contrary, less is better.

RESPONDING TO THE CLOCK

The values of a consumer society tend to be a great distortion of reality. Youth is one of the core values of the consumer agenda. Youth is not a priority in God's scheme. We all are not getting younger. That is God's plan. Otherwise the clock would be changed. We all need a lot of the freedom that May talks about when we are facing the unchanging tyrant of the clock. We often are conflicted between staying young and facing the reality of preparing for an older future.

Acceptance tells us to make financial preparations but also to be open to that aging future with its myriad encounters with our limits. Being real goes far beyond having economic security. Willingness and willfulness offer us a real challenge in being honest about the aging process.

TERESA'S PRAYER

Teresa often advised her followers to get real. She gained this gem of wisdom at the cost of much suffering. More than anything else, she experienced reality as immersed in God's loving mercy. She continually talked about herself as a world-class sinner. This was no make-believe world based on false humility. Her closeness to God brought a mystical light that illuminated her mind and heart. She saw her broken self with stunning clarity. Her perception of reality underlined her limits and shortcomings. At the same time, she experienced the basic graciousness of life in the hands of a merciful and compassionate God. Teresa's response was a full-hearted acceptance of this truth. This led her to continuously talk of God's mercy and express the fact that her story was the story of this limitless forgiveness.

Teresa's prayer is a beautiful expression of this truth of her life. Reality is awash in the mercy and love of God. Once this is grasped and accepted, it is easy to say:

May nothing disturb you.
May nothing make you afraid.
Everything passes.

Teresa's life, on the surface, was worthy of a long-running soap opera that would run an episode each week for decades. She was always "falling off a cliff," running out of money, discovering new enemies in high places and among the simple town folk. Church authorities often were ruthlessly opposed to this simple Carmelite nun.

Her basic stance of surrender in willingness set her free. She had no trouble either proclaiming or living a life of acceptance in the midst of the turmoil. She knew:

> *God alone never changes.*
> *Patience can attain anything.*
> *He who has God within lacks nothing.*

In the five steps of dying, one finally arrives at peaceful surrender in accepting the reality of death. In Teresa's prayer, we are called to the same acceptance. However, the acceptance is not of death but of life that we say yes to in peace. This life eventually opens to death as a call to paradise. We are blessed in this surrender with the beginning of heaven here and now.

> *God is enough.*

Fourteen

TERESA'S MESSAGE

Get Real!

PRAYING OUR WAY INTO LIFE

MY FAMILY WAS VERY SERIOUS ABOUT BEING CATHOLIC. I bought into the program. One of the early problems I had in this commitment was in our parish church.

There was an arch over the sanctuary. On this arch was a large painting of what I thought was a bar-b-que pit. Our patron saint, the martyr St. Laurence, was the bar-b-que wrapped up in flames. This really spooked me out, since I was taught that St. Laurence truly was a good Catholic.

At the age of eighteen I entered the Carmelites. A year later I began the novitiate where the chapel held another challenge. On the walls were little sayings from Carmelite saints of how wonderful it was to suffer. One, in particular, shook me up: it is better to suffer than to die! Then there was a picture of St. Teresa with a burning arrow piercing her heart. This led me to long for the baseball game after lunch.

These two images were characteristic of the spirituality of my pre-Vatican II upbringing. We were being called out of life to the spiritual. We separated God from life. This was a disastrous division. Life was one thing. The need to be spiritual and prayerful was truly an invitation into the otherworldly. It seemed as if the goal of our prayer was to withdraw from life.

Over time, and with the insights of Vatican II, I learned this approach of otherworldliness was totally contradictory to Teresa's message. Teresa's message is: Get real! We are, in fact, called to pray our way into life. Our problem is to discover what the true life is. Most often this call to reality is expressed in Teresa's reoccurring theme of the utter importance of humility and self-knowledge.

In the Carmelite tradition, personal purification and transformation are central. If embraced, they facilitate the destiny of every human being: union with God. A major part of this transformation is the elimination of the false consciousness that clouds and deceives all human experience. God's grace, particularly in Jesus, is calling us out of this darkness into a new light. For Teresa, this is the journey from the unreal to the real. As has been stated so often in this text, this Carmelite mystic always taught that deep personal prayer is the way forward.

In Teresa's view, prayer opens the deepest meaning and value of human existence. It is the inner life that animates and challenges a way of living permeated by frivolous and meaningless pursuits. The movement of true spirituality is from the façade to the inner core. The journey within is the passage into reality.

Take the example of a fish and water. It is impossible for the fish to see how water surrounds its reality. The fish has no platform to step outside the water to understand the water's dominance in the fish's world. In the human situation, there is a similarity in the false values created by our society, our culture, and our ego. For us, however, prayer gives us a platform to withdraw from the enclosed world of our misconceptions. Prayer beckons us to humility and self-knowledge. We pass from the bondage of the false consciousness to the real world centered on God. Prayer is the platform that opens us to liberation from our self-deception and unreality.

These insights from Teresa's message help us see:

1. We are locked into a false consciousness.

2. This false consciousness creates a worldview that is a gross distortion of reality but a worldview we mistakenly embrace as true.

3. Part of this worldview is based on the power of a society that defines us as a consumer.

4. We are bound by the deep and hidden prejudices aimed at protecting our economic, political, cultural, gender, social, and racial privileges to the exclusion and deprivation of others.

5. The ego is in a relentless struggle to avoid any diminishment of its control of our false consciousness. Teresa's teaching on the third dwelling places is especially forceful in exposing the ego's power to deceive. This is what we mean by self-absorption.

6. The passage to freedom is to "Get real."

THE GOAL IS UNION WITH GOD

The Carmelite tradition has always placed the need for transformation of the human person as the way into the most real in life, union with God. Whether it happens in this life or the next, the human heart is moving to be one with God. All that is truly real in life leads to this calling.

Teresa's message calls us to focus all our energy on the goal of being one with God. By this measure, she tells us, if it fits, keep it. If it does not, get rid of it. Prayer is the measure used to judge the authenticity of the human experience. Prayer helps us discern God's self-disclosure, drawing us into the life of God, who dwells in our deepest center.

Our invitation into transformation is God's program. God loves us first with a love that is always seeking us. Being real opens us to the divine summoning.

Teresa is emphatic that we cannot reach our true self with our own efforts. Only the activity of God in contemplation makes this final part of the journey possible. Contemplation slowly opens the reality of the overwhelming love that calls us into the real, the mystery that is God. Soon enough we learn life is of a piece. Real life and spiritual life are one. Earthly life is simply a reality that launches into eternal life. This is why John of the Cross said so profoundly, in the twilight of life only love matters.

What Teresa means when she tells us to get real is that we need to enter the process of personal transformation. Love is what we seek. We need to be purified to experience love in its truest expression. Only God can offer the real deal when it comes to love. All other authentic love is based on our participation in the divine love.

We need to change a lot of things to accept the consequences of this call to transformation and union. Jesus is God's invitation for us. Teresa insists that we place our eyes on Jesus, who is the symbol of God's passionate love for each of us. He is God's continuing invitation to loving intimacy. In this context, we learn that all of life is of concern for us. There is no separation of the holy and the ordinary. Everything that happens can help us or hurt us on this quest for the real that is union with God. Life is the greatest grace. Deep and committed personal prayer is our entry into the mystery of love.

CONCLUSION

THE HUMAN HEART IS MADE FOR LOVE. In one way or another, it will achieve this goal by being one with God. The story of salvation tells us Jesus is calling us to walk with him into the mystery of love.

The message of this text is that deep personal prayer is an essential part of this journey of walking with Jesus into life.

For better or for worse, we are going to be purified from the consequences of sin flowing from the failure of our first parents and our personal failures. This purification leading to transformation will happen. It is our choice: this life or the next life after death.

Deep personal prayer is the opportunity God gives us to become free. Deep personal prayer is the call to choose life not death. Deep personal prayer is the invitation of "get real." Deep personal prayer is the treasure that draws us into the kingdom. Deep personal prayer draws us out of darkness and isolation to a path of justice and peace and the integrity of creation. Deep personal prayer is a summons to learn true love by walking with Jesus.

QUESTIONS FOR REFLECTION

1. What is your definition of prayer?
   How has your understanding of the purpose
   of prayer changed after reading this book?

2. Why is self-knowledge important to prayer?

3. How might praying with Scripture enhance
   your prayer life?

4. How might the practice of meditative prayer deepen
   your relationship with God and others?

5. What changes in our lives when we pray regularly?

6. Do you encounter the person of Jesus Christ in your
   prayer? What might be a roadblock to meeting Jesus?

7. How might our experience of Teresa of Ávila's
   "Contemplative Switch" change our understanding
   of God?

8. Why are the three virtues—humility, detachment,
   and charity—important in contemporary culture?

9. Do you believe you are a sinner?
   Do you believe in the unending mercy of God?

10. How does a deep and ongoing prayer life prepare us
    for union with God?

OF RELATED INTEREST

Benedictine Promises for Everyday People
Staying Put, Listening Well, Being Changed by God
RACHEL M. SRUBAS

In this engaging, spiritual, and very down-to-earth book, Rachel Srubas shows us how the three promises of the followers of St. Benedict—staying put, listening well, and being changed by God—can be applied to our everyday lives, no matter our situation.
136 PAGES | $14.95 | 5½" X 8½" | 9781627854412

The Grace of Patience
Discovering the Spiritual Abundance of Waiting
MARGARET WHIPP

Having to wait is a fact of life. In this beautifully written book, Margaret Whipp explores several kinds of waiting and shows how each can become a moment of grace in our lives. She offers helpful activities and exercises to turn these moments of disquiet into prayerful encounters with calm and peace.
112 PAGES | $12.95 | 5½" X 8½" | 9781627853651

On Becoming Bread
Reflections and Stories to Nourish Your Spirit
DR. MARY MARROCCO

On Becoming Bread is an inspiring companion for anyone seeking to discover how God is present in every moment of our lives. Steeped equally in Scripture, sound theology, each reflection reveals new dimensions of the most ordinary of day-to-day events.
128 PAGES | $14.95 | 5½" X 8½" | 9781627854443

TO ORDER CALL 1-800-321-0411
OR VISIT WWW.TWENTYTHIRDPUBLICATIONS.COM

TWENTY-THIRD PUBLICATIONS
A division of Bayard, Inc.